100

INDOOR
GAMES
for SCHOOL KIDS

Games! Games! Games! The ideas in this book will add a new dimension of fun to your time with school kids, no matter what setting you are in! And these games aren't just for fun; playing games with your school-age kids will reinforce what they are learning. Kids will learn *even better* when they are actively involved. As you use these games you'll be amazed at the fun kids can have while they praise God and learn more about His word.

100 INDOOR GAMES FOR SCHOOL KIDS

Cook Ministry Resources
a division of Cook Communications Ministries
Colorado Springs, Colorado/Paris, Ontario

© 1997 Cook Ministry Resources
a division of Cook Communications Ministries
4050 Lee Vance View
Colorado Springs, CO 80918-7100

Editor: Janna McCasland
Designer: Sonya Duckworth

Printed in the United States of America
ISBN: 0-7814-5331-3

CONTENTS

ICE BREAKERS

1 *Detective*

In advance: Prepare 4" x 6" pieces of paper by attaching a picture and/or name of each child to the paper. (Names will suffice but pictures are more fun.)

Children line up side by side so the leader can tape a paper to each child's back without the child seeing it. When everyone is ready, the children begin to mingle, asking each other questions that can be answered with a "yes" or a "no" answer. For example, "Does my person have red hair?" "Is my person a girl?" When a child is ready to guess the identity of the person on his or her back, he or she tells the leader. The leader confirms or denies it. If the guess is wrong, the child continues asking questions. If the guess is correct, the child may still participate by answering other players' questions. The game is over when everyone has discovered his or her mystery person.

2 *Easter Home Run*

(John 19—20)

In advance: Write out questions from the Scriptures, relating to Easter. Write out *single, double, triple,* or *home run* in the corner of the card, depending on the question's difficulty. On the back of the card put the matching answer. Divide all children into two teams. Arrange four chairs into a diamond shape, like bases for baseball. The first player on a team sits in the chair designated as home base. The leader asks a question saying whether it's a single, double, etc. Then if a player correctly answers the question, they can move that number of bases. If the answer is wrong, the player gets a strike. Three strikes means that player is out and the next player on the team gets to try. After three outs the next team has a turn at bat. Runs are recorded by the leader. The winner is the team with the most runs when twenty minutes are up—or set a number of innings to play!

3 *Puzzles! Puzzles! Puzzles!*

Write out the words to several verses on different colored pieces of tagboard and then cut them into puzzle pieces. Distribute puzzle pieces randomly to children and instruct them to find others with puzzle pieces of the same color. Children work together to assemble their puzzles and may then either (1) say the verse together for the class, (2) name a way they can obey the verse, or (3) pantomime a way to obey the verse.

4 *Who Am I?*

Distribute paper and pencils to the participants. Have them write one true thing about themselves that they do not think anyone knows. An example is, "I was born with a tooth!" Collect the papers in a basket and draw them one at a time, reading the contents to the group. Group members guess which child matches the statement. When the owner is identified, give the child an opportunity to explain or expand on their statement if desired.

5 *An Egg-cellent Adventure*

Give each child a raw egg. Let them use colored markers to turn the egg into an "egg-cellent" model of themselves. Be sure everyone signs their name on their egg. Have the children sit in a circle and show their eggs to the others in the group. Then cover the floor with a large plastic sheet and have the children form a line, each about two feet from the next. Put all of the eggs in a basket at one end of the line. Place the empty basket at the other end. The object of the game is to move the eggs from one basket to another by tossing them from child to child. If an egg is dropped, the child who decorated it must drop out of the line, leaving one place vacant. The remaining players must toss the eggs across the empty space. Continue until all eggs have been tossed.

6 *Bind Us Together, Lord*

In advance: Using camp spoons that have a hole in the handle, tie each spoon securely to the loose end of a ball of yarn.

Have the children form two lines. Give one spoon to the child at the end of each line. The child threads the yarn though his or her clothing (in one sleeve, out another; down the pants leg; etc.), then passes the spoon to the next in line, who repeats the process. The winner is the first team to be totally "bound" together. To remove the yarn, cut the spoon off and pull from the yarn ball end. (Warning! It tickles!)

7 *Sixth Day Safari!*

In advance: Cut postcards with animal pictures into jigsaw puzzles. Make a simple puzzle for younger children, and a more complicated puzzle for older children. Hide the pieces around the room.

As they enter the room give each child a piece of one picture. Let them search for the other pieces. If they find a piece that does not fit their puzzle, they must leave it face up on a table or desk. The winner is the first child to finish his or her puzzle and tape it on a piece of construction paper. This game can be played in teams—just give each team one puzzle piece to begin.

8 *Walking on Eggshells*

In advance: Lay a large, washable tarp out on the floor. Place piles of whipping cream and globs of cold, flavored gelatin randomly on the tarp. Place large clean towels and buckets of water at the end of the tarp.
Divide students into two to four groups, (not boys against girls—voices must be mixed!) and have them remove

their socks and shoes. One student from each team is blindfolded, and turned around three times. They start at the same time from one end of the tarp. The goal is to reach the other side without stepping in something icky. Teams may call directions to their blindfolded player, but cannot call the player by name. The goal is for the child to learn to distinguish the voices of his or her own team in order to make it safely to the other side.

9 *Wonderful You*

Have children sit in a large circle. The leader begins a clapping rhythm: clap-clap, knee-slap, snap-snap, palms out. To this rhythm each child—one at a time—recites the following phrase and fills in the blank with a rhyme: "She's a wonderful person. We call her Pam. I like her 'cause she _____." Ideas might include: "—won't eat ham," "— rides a tram," "—is a lamb," etc. The rhymes can be silly or serious. Continue around the circle using each child's name. This is a noncompetitive game. If a child can't think of a rhyme, anyone else may call out an idea.

10 *Draw it!*

On index cards, write the numbers 1-6. Make six cards for each number. The object of the game is to be the first to draw a complete person while getting to know others. To draw a Christian, a player must draw:

> Two 1's—(Head and Body)
> Two 2's—(Arms)
> Two 3's—(Legs)
> One 4—(Mouth)
> Two 5's—(Eyes)
> One 6—(Heart and Cross)

Each person takes a turn choosing two cards from the pile. (Kids can choose any cards, not necessarily the top two.) After choosing two cards, the player tells one thing about him or herself and then draws the part of the body that correlates with the cards chosen. The cards are then shuffled back into the card pile. When a player chooses a card with numbers that cannot be used, the next player takes a turn until someone has drawn a complete person.

11 *True or False*

Children take turns writing three statements about themselves on a chalk board or flip chart for the group to see—two true and one false. (If your kids are young, have them say the statements rather than write them.) The group must then try to figure out which statements are true and which one is false. Have the children raise their hands to make their guesses about the statements. After hearing from a number of children, let the child give the correct answer and a short explanation of the statements. Children who guess correctly which statements are true and which are false, can be the next to come up and write their own statements.

12 *Getting to Know You*

In advance: Make information sheets with ten simple fill-in questions. Some ideas are: Who —has a brother? —has blond hair? —can rollerblade?

Distribute the papers and pencils. Inform the children that they have five minutes to fill in the blanks by getting the signature of someone who matches a certain description. Some of the information can be seen (blond hair). Other information cannot be discovered without asking several people the question. The children should try to have a different child's signature on each line.

After five minutes, gather the children together. Have each child introduce one other child to the group by saying the child's name and something about him or her.

13 *The Name Game*

Children stand in a large circle and state their first names. One child is "It" and stands in the center of the circle holding a pillow. "It" uses the pillow to tag players who cannot quickly recall others' names. Begin the game by calling out your own name, then someone else's name. The child whose name was just called, quickly states his or her own name and another name before being tagged. Any child who is tagged becomes "It." He or she must take the pillow, come to the center of the circle and begin play by saying his or her own name and the name of another child in the circle. If the kids need a name refresher, stop the game and go around the circle once more, having each child state his or her name.

14 *Acrostic Antics*

Have each child write the letters of his or her name verti-
cally down the side of a sheet of paper. They should then
think of words or phrases that describe themselves which
begin with each letter of their name. (Note the examples
below.) Have the children take turns sharing their acros-
tics with the group, explaining why they chose the words
they did.

P arks
A lways thinking
U nderstanding
L unch

C ats
A ctive
T rusting
H orses
Y oung

BIBLE STORIES

15 *Jesus in the Temple*

Play this game after telling the story of Mary and Joseph losing track of the boy Jesus on their trip back from Jerusalem (Matthew 2:16-32 and Luke 2:40-52). Hide a picture of Jesus somewhere in the building. Let the children divide into pairs representing Mary and Joseph. Explain the boundaries in the building where the children may go looking for Jesus. For younger children: when a pair has found Jesus, the pair brings the picture or doll back to the group. They get to hide it next. For older children: when a pair of children finds Jesus, they come to the group leader and whisper the location in the leader's ear to confirm it. Then they can give clues to the pairs still searching until everyone finds it.

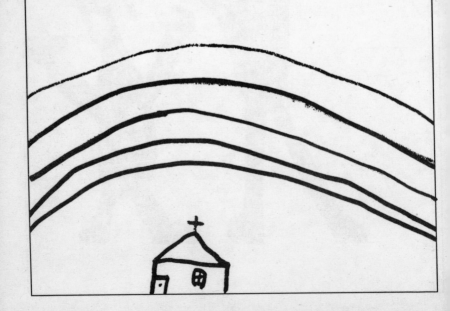

16 *Joseph's Cup*

(Genesis 44:1—45:5)

In advance: Use spray paint or gold glitter to decorate one paper cup to be Joseph's royal cup. Stand up identical paper grocery bags so there is one per child and put the gold cup in one bag and plain cups in the others. Fold the tops of the bags over twice.

Select one child to be Joseph and one to be his servant. The other children, "Joseph's brothers," stand around them in a circle holding the bags. While Joseph claps his hands in a rhythm, the brothers pass the bags around the circle. When Joseph stops clapping, each player looks in the bag he is holding but tries not to reveal whether he has the golden cup or not. Joseph's servant gets three tries to guess who has the cup. Whoever has the cup becomes the next Joseph and chooses a servant.

17 *David and Goliath*

This is a game from Mexico which can be adapted for many themes by substituting other words for "David" and "Goliath" (1 Samuel 17:28-48). Examples: Mary and

Martha (Luke 10:38-42), bread and fish (John 6:1-15), ship and whale (Jonah 1:1-17), manna and quail (Exodus 16:11-17).

Select two children and let them secretly choose to be David or Goliath. These two children hold hands and make an arch over a 3' masking tape line on the floor. The rest of the children line up to walk under the arch. Play a music cassette or CD for about one minute. When the music stops, the children making the arch drop their arms and trap whoever is under the arch. The captured player whispers "David" or "Goliath" to the two arch makers. He is secretly told which child is the person he has chosen (so no one else hears), and the player goes to stand behind the chosen person with his hands on the waist of the leader.

The line of children resumes marching under the arch when the music starts. Each person who is caught in the arch quietly chooses David or Goliath and stands behind the appropriate leader, creating two chains of children. When all the children have been caught, one option is to have a tug of war between the two teams. The teams can play by holding on to the waist of the person in front of them, or by pulling on a rope. The team which pulls the other team across the tape line is the winner.

18 *Love in Action*

This game is based on the command of 1 John 3:18 to love others with our actions, not just our words. It could also be used to teach the Golden Rule from Luke 6:31.

This game is similar to a board game, but the children are the markers as well as the players. Make a spinner by dividing a piece of paper into six sections labeled with the numbers 1-6. Put a paper fastener through the center of the page, with a paper clip secured between the fastener and the paper. Bend the prongs of the fastener back but leave it loose enough that the paper clip can spin on top of the paper. Create a playing "board" by making a path with colored sheets of paper that winds around the room. Use at least 40 papers in the path, or more if you like. Mark the first paper "Start" and the last "Finish." Tape the papers to the floor with masking tape. Have children stand at "start." Let kids take turns spinning a number and moving themselves that number of spaces on the path. After each child has gone once, say, "Now, if anyone spins a six, you get to choose someone behind you in the game to come up and stand with you, then you both get to move forward six spaces. If you're the last person in the game, you get to move six spaces, then choose anyone else to go forward two spaces." Continue playing until all children have finished the game, then talk about how it felt to help others win.

19 *In the Belly of a Fish*

This game is to be played with the story of Jonah. In advance: paint a large paper or canvas bag to look like a great fish of the deep: eye balls, fins, purple spots, whatever!

Choose two students to help with the fish. The rest of the students start on one side of the room. The leader stands across the room (in Nineveh), and gives commands such as, "The Master says, 'Take two hops toward Nineveh.'" If any student moves on a command not preceded by, "the Master says," the helpers bring out the fish. Saying, "Glub, glub, burble, swish! You go to Nineveh in the belly of a fish!" they put the bag over the child who moved and lead him or her to the Nineveh wall. You might have a prize for the students who make it to Nineveh without being swallowed, and a gummy worm for each of the students who traveled by fish!

20 *Noah's Noisy Neighbors*

(Genesis 6:17-22)

In advance: Make 3" x 5" file cards representing these animals (pictures for preschoolers, or words for readers): pig, duck, dog, cat, cow, lion, sheep, or other animals whose sounds are easily made and recognized by children. Make four cards for each animal. You need to have as many cards as you have children, plus four more cards for variety. Place the cards in a grocery bag. With chalk, masking tape or a rope, mark off an ark-shaped area on the floor for the finish point, or hang a picture of the ark on a wall for the winners to tag.

After telling the story of Noah from Genesis 6:17-22, have each child pick a card, read it, and put it face down in a discard pile. When the leader, "Noah," gives the signal, all the children crawl around making their animals' sounds. The children try to form a group of their kind of animal. Depending on which cards were picked, there may be 2, 3, or 4 of each kind of animal. When a group of animals is sure they have all their members, they race to the ark. The first group there is the winner, provided they have all their members.

Option for older children: have them do this game blindfolded or with their eyes shut. When a group of animals is sure they have all their members, they should stand and open their eyes. If they are the first complete group, Noah declares them the winners.

21 *Mr. and Mrs. Noah's Trip*

Divide all children into two lines and have them sit down and remove their shoes. The leader will collect all the shoes and put them in a pile a few feet from both lines. Place robes and beards in the pile for boys to dress as "Mr. Noah." and robes and necklaces in a pile for girls to dress as "Mrs. Noah." When the leader yells "Go!" the first child on each team runs to the pile, finds his or her own pair of shoes, puts on a Mr. or Mrs. Noah outfit and runs back to the next person on the team. The next person puts on the robe and must find his or her own pair of shoes and a beard or necklace in the pile before running back to tag the next person. The first team to be seated with all members wearing their shoes wins the relay.

22 *Manna Mania*

After discussing the manna in the wilderness (Exodus 16:13-36) divide your group into two teams. Set an easy-to-cut candy bar on a plate for each team. Have a plastic knife and fork for each team member. At the "go" signal the first person on each team puts on a pair of mittens, runs to the table, unwraps the candy bar, picks up a plastic knife and fork, cuts and eats a slice from the candy bar. That child then returns to his or her team, and gives the mittens to the next person in line who proceeds in the same manner. Have extra candy bars available if needed. The first team whose members have all eaten from the candy bar is the winner.

23 *Lazarus Is Alive!*

After studying the story of Lazarus (John 11:1-44), divide the group into several teams. Each team selects one person to be Lazarus. The teams are given one roll of toilet paper and are instructed to wrap their Lazarus, being careful not to break the toilet paper until their roll is completely gone. When each team uses an entire roll they watch and cheer on their Lazarus as he proceeds to hop, twirl or lay down and roll, being careful not to tear the paper. Lazarus continues to unwrap himself by turning around and around or doing whatever is necessary to accomplish his/her goal. The team with the longest unbroken section of paper wins.

24 *Run, David, Run*

Ask one volunteer to be "David" and another "Saul." Divide the rest of the children into two teams of David's men, and differentiate between the teams by giving them names or numbers. Blindfold Saul and have him or her stand in the middle of the room. The others will quietly distribute themselves along the four walls of the room. After counting to twenty, Saul will try to "catch" David by pointing to the wall where he or she thinks the most people are. If David is against that wall, a new David and Saul are chosen. If not, all those along that wall must sit down. The rest will move quietly to different walls and Saul will try again. The team with the most people standing when David is caught, wins.

25 *Scroll Hunt*

Show a scroll made from rolled paper and string to the children. Tell them the Bible story of Josiah who found the Book of the Law (2 Kings 22:1-13). Have a volunteer leave the room. The rest of the class hides the scroll, with a little of it showing. Call the searcher in and have him or her search for the scroll. As soon as the searcher finds the scroll, have the rest of the kids line up behind him or her and pass the scroll alternately over the head and through the legs to the back of the line. When the last person in line gets it, he or she must run to the front of the line where the leader is standing and say, "We have found the Book of the Law." That child then becomes the next searcher. As an optional challenge, time the group to see how long it takes them to find, pass, and present the scroll.

26 *Loaves and Fishes*

In advance: Write out the names of several types of bread and fish on large slips of paper. (Fish: Goldfish, Sun Fish, Trout, Walleye, Carp, Angelfish, Bullhead. Bread: Whole Wheat, White, Pumpernickel, Rye, Caraway, French, Sourdough.) Hide them throughout the room.

Divide the group into two teams—fish and bread. At the signal, each team will collect as many slips of paper representing their category as possible. Each time a slip is found it may be added to the team basket. Any slip for the other team must be left in its hiding place. When the leader calls time, count the number of slips in each basket. The team with the most bread or fish wins. Tell the story of Jesus feeding the 5,000 from Mark 6:30-44.

27 *Twelve Spies*

After studying the twelve spies (Numbers 13:1-25) divide the children into teams. Have a pair of 36" two-by-fours for each team. Attach two hand straps (36" long strings), and two strings long enough to serve as foot straps, to each board. Place a bowl of grapes and an empty bowl for each team on a table, 10 feet from a starting point. The first player for each team puts his or her feet into the foot straps, holds the long straps taut, and walks from the starting point to the table. He or she then places the end of a straw against a grape, sucks in to hold the grape in place, and deposits the grape into the empty bowl. (A dropped grape may not be picked up.) The players must then walk back to the starting point and give the boards to the next child. Play continues until all have played. The team with the most grapes moved from one bowl to another wins.

28 *Storm at Sea*

This game correlates with the story of Jonah's disobedience as he is on a ship in a great storm (Jonah 1). It could also go with any Bible story that involves a storm at sea such as in Matthew 8 and Acts 27:18.

Arrange all the players in chairs in a circle, except for one player who is selected to be in the center. That child calls "toss right" (or "toss left") and tries to get to an empty seat as all the players move seats in the direction that is called. Play continues as the children are directed to toss right or left. Occasionally the child should call, "Storm at sea!" At this point all of the children should get up and find a new seat. When the child in the center gets a seat, the player who is left without a seat becomes the new caller.

29 *Fruit of the Spirit*

(Galatians 6:22)
Put several grapefruit-sized balloons in a cardboard box. Write a different fruit of the Spirit on each balloon. Divide the children into four groups. At

the "go" signal each team helps their captain put on baggy slacks and a large tee-shirt. The teammates then run to the box, grab balloons, run back, and stuff the balloons into their captain's shirt or pants. When the balloon box is empty the captains remove the balloons to see which team has the most unbroken balloons and the most variety of fruit of the Spirit represented. The team with the most in both categories wins.

30 *Ark Bingo*

Divide the kids into two teams and give each team a poster board that has a 16-square bingo board drawn on it. Each team brainstorms animals to put in their "ark." They write the name of one animal in each square. They can also place one Noah anywhere on the board. (He is a free place.) Teams do not show their boards to each other. When both teams are finished, team one calls out the name of an animal. If team two has that animal in any square, they can put an X on the box. It is then team two's turn to name an animal. The first team to have an X in all of the squares in any line across, diagonal, or up and down wins.

31 *ABC Animals*

Whether talking about Noah or the creation account, this is a fun memory game. Arrange the players in a circle. The leader begins by saying, "Noah took two ants into the ark." (Insert any animal, bird, or insect name that begins with the letter "a.") The next player repeats what the leader said, and adds something that begins with the letter "b." Continue this activity as consecutive players repeat the previous words and add an additional word for their new letter. It will be a challenge for everyone to remember all the words that have been given!

32 *Fruit in the Garden*

This game relates to the story of fruit trees in Genesis 1:11, and the Garden of Eden in Genesis 2:9. Arrange all the players in chairs in a circle, except for one player who is selected to stand in the center. Give each player a name of a fruit. If there are several players, give the same fruit name to two players. The player in the center, "It," should call the names of two or more fruits. Players with those fruit names must get up and change seats. At the same time, "It" tries to get an empty seat. The person who does not find a seat becomes "It."

33 *Widow's Mite*

After a discussion of the story of the widow's mite (Luke 21:1-3), divide the group into two teams. On a table, spread out several dollars worth of pennies. At the "go" signal the first person on each team runs to the table, puts a plastic sandwich bag over his/her hand, picks up a penny, and puts it in the team's basket. That child then runs back and gives the sandwich bag to the next person in line who proceeds to take his or her turn picking up a penny. Play continues until all the pennies are picked up. The team with the most money collected wins, or time the kids to see how quickly they can get all the pennies into the baskets.

BIBLE TIMES

34 *Orange Pull*

Children in Bible times made up many of their own games and toys. This is an ancient game that children might have played when Jesus was a boy. Divide the children into two or more relay teams. Give each team an orange and a five-foot piece of string. Tie small loops on both ends of the strings. Line up the teams in columns facing a goal line that is at least six to eight feet away. Place an orange on the floor in front of each team and give the first person on each team a length of string. Demonstrate how to pull the orange toward the goal line by holding the loops at the ends of the string in each hand. Loop the main part of the string around the orange and pull it toward the line. Explain that when a player gets the orange across the goal line, the orange should be picked up and quickly carried back to the next member of the team. The object of the game is to be the first team to have all of its members get the orange across the goal line and back.

35 *Wardrobe Relay*

This Bible-time simulation will be a fun way to make the children aware of the type of things people in Bible times may have worn. Divide the class into two teams and line them up behind a starting line, placing a bathrobe, a pair of sandals, a towel, and a rope or cord by the first member of each team. At the leader's signal, the first member puts on the bathrobe and sandals and arranges the towel as a headdress with the rope or cord holding it in place. The child then walks, skips, or hops to a designated turning point and back and then takes off the costume items. Each team member repeats this pattern until all have had a turn. The first team to finish wins.

36 *Prophet, Priest, King*

In advance: On separate sheets of paper, write the name of a Bible character that matches with one of these suggested Bible-time categories: Prophet (Moses, Samuel, Jeremiah); Priest (Zachariah, Caiphus, Aaron); King (David, Solomon, Herod); Judge (Samson, Gideon, Deborah); Disciple (Peter, James, John); Patriarch (Abraham, Isaac, Jacob, etc.). Make one sheet of paper for each child. Tape a different sheet to each person's back, including the category names that link the players together.

Instruct individuals to mingle and find out who they are by asking other players questions that can be answered only with "Yes" or "No." Once they have figured out their own identity, they must find the others who fit in their category.

37 *Sheep, Wolves, and Shepherds*

In advance: Inflate some balloons, and tie a short length of yarn around the knot.

Divide the group into three teams— sheep, wolves, and shepherds. Create a center line in the playing area. Have sheep stand in rows on one side of the line, with wolves on the other. Tie the string and balloon around the ankles of wolves, making sure the string is short enough so that tripping is not a hazard. During this game, sheep "baaa;" Wolves "growl." At the signal from the leader, the shepherds enter the playing area at the center line. The goal for the shepherds is to burst the balloons of the wolves before the wolves can tag the sheep. Wolves whose balloons pop must leave the game. Sheep who are tagged by wolves must also leave. All players may cross the center line, but until wolves have broken through the line of shepherds, it is probably safer to stay behind the line.

38 *Follow the Shepherd*

In advance: Mark two boundaries with masking tape, about 30" apart. The area in between these two boundary lines will be "the pasture."

Divide the class into two teams. Have each team stand single file behind one boundary. They are the "sheep" and the leader is the "shepherd." When the shepherd gives a command, such as "walk," the first sheep on each team will walk to the opposite boundary and back. They will tag the first sheep in line, who will then follow the shepherd's command. Sheep sit down in "the pasture" after their turn. The shepherd should change commands often, using different movements. The relay is over when all the sheep on one team are in the pasture.

39 *Way Back When*

Write activities that people did in Bible times on index cards. (Grind grain, get water from a well, shepherd, fish, pitch a tent, etc.) Divide the children into two groups. Play a type of charades where one child picks a card and acts out the activity. The team has one minute to guess what it is. If they cannot guess, the other team gets a chance. Continue play until all the cards have been used.

40 *Mail Relay*

This game is a Bible-time activity simulation. It would work well with stories where messages are circulated, especially with the letters of Paul. In advance: Write the names of four Bible places on separate sheets of colored paper.

Tape the prepared signs to the shirts of four volunteers. Then line the rest of the group into two equal teams and have them line up several yards from the volunteers. Give the first person in each team an envelope. These players will race to deliver the "mail" to place #1 and return to tag their next teammate who will run to take the letter from place #1 and deliver it to place #2. Continue and repeat through the four places until one team wins by being the first to have all players carry the mail.

41 *Navigation Cooperation*

In advance: Lay newspaper on the floor in a boat shape with edges touching, one page for every two children. If your class is large, make more boats. Also scatter a number of items such as toy whales, fish, anchors, nets, etc. on the floor of the room.

To play, kids must stand on the newspaper boat and work together (with or without a time limit) to collect the items you designate that are floating on the water (the floor of the room). To propel the boat, the back person will step on the paper in front of him or her, pick up the free paper, and pass it up to the boat's bow (or side, if turning). The children will have to adjust their positions to stay on the papers, direct the boat, and straighten it after turns.

42 *God's Army*

In advance: On four separate index cards write *North, South, East,* and *West.* Tape each card to a wall. Put a strip of masking tape on the floor for each team's home base. Use this game with any Bible story about soldiers or battles. Stories about Old Testament people such as Gideon (Judges 7) or David are good options. Divide the class into teams. Each team will gather at a home base. When the leader calls, "Charge!" all children run to any wall they choose. When the leader calls, "North!" all children run to the wall marked north. The last two children to reach the north wall sit down at their team's home base. If the leader calls, "Surrender!" all children fall to the floor. The leader keeps calling directions until only one child is left. That child can then take the leader's place and begin calling out the directions.

43 *Float the Boat*

Divide the kids into groups of four or five and give each group a roll of masking tape. Assign each group part of a fishing scene (boat, water, net, shoreline, fish, etc.). Each group will create their part of the scene by putting masking tape on the floor in that particular design. Give the children a time limit to complete the whole scene. When each group does its part, the final product will look great!

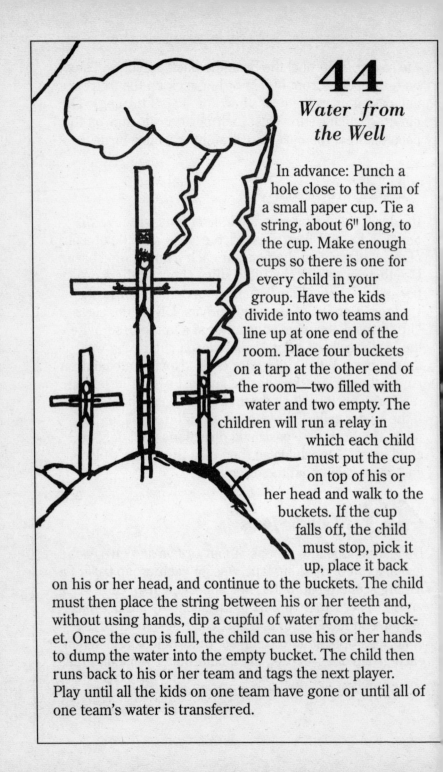

44
Water from the Well

In advance: Punch a hole close to the rim of a small paper cup. Tie a string, about 6" long, to the cup. Make enough cups so there is one for every child in your group. Have the kids divide into two teams and line up at one end of the room. Place four buckets on a tarp at the other end of the room—two filled with water and two empty. The children will run a relay in which each child must put the cup on top of his or her head and walk to the buckets. If the cup falls off, the child must stop, pick it up, place it back on his or her head, and continue to the buckets. The child must then place the string between his or her teeth and, without using hands, dip a cupful of water from the bucket. Once the cup is full, the child can use his or her hands to dump the water into the empty bucket. The child then runs back to his or her team and tags the next player. Play until all the kids on one team have gone or until all of one team's water is transferred.

ALL ABOUT CHURCH

45 *Caterpillar Caper*

In advance: Mark a starting line along one side of the room, and a finish line along the opposite side, using masking tape, chalk, or rope.

This game represents the way the church is meant to function, with many members working together toward a common goal. You could share Romans 15:5-6, Romans 12:4-5, and/or Philippians 2:2-4. Divide the group into teams of three to six players. Each team sits in a row behind the starting line with knees bent and feet flat on the floor. Each child places his or her hands on the ankles of the child behind him or her. At the leader's signal, each team tries to move forward as a unit by lifting all their feet (held by the hands) forward at one time. Then they shift their weight to their feet/hands in order to lift and scoot all their hips forward simultaneously. Continue moving feet, then hips, then feet, etc. The winning team is the first one to completely cross the finish line.

46 *Mission Shuffleboard*

In advance: Fill some plastic milk cartons half full of sand and tape them shut. Choose a colored permanent marker for each team. Mark a large shuffleboard court on the floor using masking tape. Write the name of a country on a 3" x 5" card in each space on the shuffleboard court.

Divide the group into teams. One child kneels on a skateboard (hold on!) and is pushed from a starting line toward the shuffle board. Only one push is allowed. If the skateboard doesn't reach the shuffleboard court, then it is the other team's turn. If the child does reach the court, plant a milk carton "church" in that square. Be sure to put a dot on the carton with that team's color so that they can tell which churches belong to their team. The other team then tries to plant a "church." If a "church" is knocked over by a child on a skateboard, it is removed from the board. The winner is the team with the most "churches" at the end of the game.

47 *Build the Church*

In advance: Make some construction paper squares out of colored paper. Divide the group into pairs. Give each pair the same number of squares (at least 20). When the leader gives the signal, pairs work together to build their own church made of the construction paper squares by propping the squares against each other. The first pair to complete their church construction by using all of the squares, wins.

48 *Church-Grams*

A leader reads the letters of the
word "church." The rest
of the group is to write a
Christian message using
these letters as the first
letter of each word in the
message. One point is awarded for
each letter that is used in the
church-gram. Allow three minutes
for each church-gram creation.
(Some examples of phrases to give
the kids are, "Christ loves you,"
"Hold on to the promises of God,"
etc.) After players have finished
making their church-grams, have
volunteers take turns reading
them out loud.

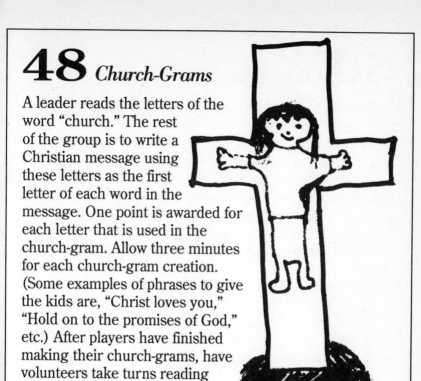

49 *Scripture Word Search*

Divide the class into two teams. Each team selects a captain. The captain comes to the front of the room, and selects a word or name from the Bible that their team must locate. (They have to find the word somewhere in the Bible but not necessarily where the captain found it.) After the word has been found, one team member races to the captain, revealing their finding. One point is awarded for a correct finding. That person then takes the captain's place and the previous captain joins the rest of the team.

50 *Church Bingo*

Make a list of words on the chalkboard that have to do with church (preacher, Bible, songs, cross, etc.) Use more words than spaces. Give each child a pencil and a piece of paper divided into 16 equal sections. Have children put the words on their grid in any order they choose. Leave one square blank. Use buttons for markers and have children cover the blank square with a button. Then call the words, one at a time. The first person that gets a full row says "Church!" The winner tells something about at least one word that was covered. Clear the cards and play again. Children may want to exchange cards after a few rounds.

51 *Prayer Flags*

Draw an international flag on each index card. On the back of each card, write a fact and prayer request for the nation represented. Cut the flags in half using zigzag patterns. Distribute half a flag to each child. Children mingle to find the partner who can complete their flag. When they find their "match," children sit in pairs and read the cards. Have a world map available so the kids can locate the country they have on their cards. Pray in partners or as a large group.

52 *Church Board Game*

Make "Quiz Cards" containing questions relating to recent lesson topics. Make four cards each with the words related to church (listed below). Make four game pieces and four tokens to move along the board. Create a game board that has spaces labeled *Sunday school, church, worship, pray,* and *sing.* Make up labels for other spaces on the board Quiz Card, and leave some spaces blank. Place scraps of paper with the numbers 1-6 written on them in a basket. Two to four players take turns moving along the game board by drawing a number and moving that number of spaces. They can choose to move forward or backward on any turn. When they land on a space labeled Quiz Card, they must answer a question correctly before moving on. When a player lands on a space labeled with one of the words relating to church, the player collects a card for that word. The first child to obtain a card for *Sunday school, church, worship, pray,* and *sing,* wins!

53 *Come to Church!*

This game is a variation of "Red Light, Green Light." Choose one student to be the "pastor" and have the rest of the students stand on the opposite side of the room. The "pastor" should say, "Come to church!" and turn his or her back to the group. When the "pastor" turns and faces the group, they must stop. If the "pastor" sees anyone still moving, that child must go back to the starting point. The child who reaches the "pastor" first gets to be the "pastor" for the next round.

54 *Fingerprint Church*

Talk with the kids about the fact that we often think of the church as the building, but it is the people who are the church. Each person in the church is a special individual, different from everyone else. Divide the kids into teams of six and give each team a stamp pad, a piece of white paper, and a damp cloth or paper towel. At the signal, the children are to use their fingerprints to make a picture of the church building. Tell the kids that they have four minutes to plan and make their picture. When time is up have the kids clean off their hands and then compare the pictures. See how different the buildings are as well as the different fingerprints that made them.

CHARACTER BUILDERS

55 *Balloony-Ball*

This game encourages children to work together. Use it to help them learn more about teamwork, or working together as the body of Christ. Mark a center line down the middle of the floor with masking tape. Designate one side "A" and the other side "B." Inflate several balloons and set them aside. Form two groups and have children sit on the floor. Explain that the rules of the game are similar to volleyball, with teams trying to get a balloon to the other team's side of the court with only three hits per side. However, there are several additional rules:

• Players must remain fully seated during the game.
• Players on side A may only use one hand. They must keep the other hand on the floor at all times.
• Players on side B may only use their feet. Hands may not be used.

Begin playing and keep score as in volleyball. Use extra balloons if the playing balloon pops. When one team reaches 10 points, have kids switch handicaps, then continue play.

56 *Trust Train*

In advance: Write this rhyme in large print on a chalkboard or poster so everyone can see it:

**We're on our way to heaven
And we're never turning back!**

**We'll trust and follow Jesus
So we're on the right track!**

Choose one child to be the engine and let him or her choose the first "caboose" to wear a blindfold. All the other children join hands in a circle and lift their arms, making arches. The caboose puts his or her hands on the engine's shoulders and follows the engine in and out of the arches while everyone says the rhyme one time. On the last word, the train stops. The caboose removes the blindfold and hands it to the child nearest him. That child puts on the blindfold and joins the train as the new "caboose." (The leader can fill in when needed to complete an arch.) The train continues as the children repeat the rhyme. The game ends when there is only one arch left. The players making that arch become the next leader and caboose.

57 *Go for the Goal!*

This is a marathon relay that can be used to teach children about persevering to reach goals by helping one another. (Taken from 1 Corinthians 9:24.) Using chalk, make a large circle. Then put a long strip of tape across part of the circle for the start/finish line. Place two caps in the center of the circle. Divide all children into two teams behind the start line. Each team is given a baton (plastic diving stick or paper towel tube). When the

leader says "Go for the goal!" the first runner on each team will run two laps around the circle and then pass the baton to the next runner on the team. The last runner must go two laps before entering the middle of the circle and placing a cap on his or her head. The team then stands in a line and passes the hat from head to head. When everyone on the team has worn the hat, the whole team sits down.

58 Communication Draw-Backs

In advance: Prepare simple illustrations of a variety of images, symbols, words, etc. These may be related to any theme. For example, "Praise God" might include guitar, sheet of music, praying hands, Bible, etc.

Form two or more teams. Each team should sit in a line, side by side, with shoulders touching. Place a flip chart or chalkboard at the front of the room. Show a picture to the child on each team who is farthest from the board. They must draw this picture in the palm of the hand of the person sitting in front of them using only one finger. In this way the drawing is passed up to the front of each group. Finally, the person closest to the board draws what he or she thinks the image is, for all to see. Then show the original picture and see how close they came. Rotate players from the front to the back and continue with the next illustration.

59 Fruit-of-the-Spirit Dominos

(Galatians 5:22-25)
In advance: Write the following fruits of the Spirit on index cards, one word per card, using each word at least two times: love, joy, peace, patience, kindness, goodness,

faithfulness, gentleness, self-control. To determine the number of cards you will need, multiply the number of players by two. Divide that number by nine, and you will know how many cards to make for each word.

The children pick two cards each and become "human dominos" by taping one card to their forehead and one to their ankles. Ask one child to start the game by lying down in the middle of a circle made by the other children. Whoever can match one of the fruits on the first "domino" should quickly raise his or her hand. The first child to do this is recognized by the leader, then lies down so the matching word card is next to the first domino's word. Play proceeds like a regular domino game, except matches are possible at any end or corner of the arrangement of dominoes. The goal is for the whole group to cooperate in such a way that all the players find a place to fit together.

60 *Human Pinball Machine*

Have children sit in a semicircle facing a wall, with their legs spread, and their feet touching. (The last child on each side of the semicircle should have one foot against the wall.) Place a large box against the wall, open end toward the children. Have each student clasp his hands over his or her head, and lean over to form a human paddle. The leader rolls a ball into the group. The object of the game is to bat the ball into the box. If the ball stalls in the middle, the leader can kick it toward the students. Talk about the importance of working as one to accomplish the purpose of getting the ball into the box.

61 *Follow Directions Volleyball*

In advance: Set up a volleyball net at ground level and inflate a large beach ball. Divide the students into two teams. Have the children remove their shoes and lay on their backs with their feet in the air. The only one allowed to stand is the server, who uses an under-hand lob to get the ball over the net. The children on the other team must kick it back over the net. The leader calls out different directions for the kids to follow as they play. Here are some ideas: Players use only their right foot; spin around on your back once while the ball is on the other team's side; clap twice before kicking the ball; everyone sings a song while playing; etc. Directions can be crazy for added fun!

62 *Promise Cubes*

Give each person a paper cube to mark (made by folding paper and taping the sides). The children should write the words or draw a symbol for the following categories on each side of the cube:
1) YOU—A promise you have made to someone else
2) Smiling face—A promise you have made to yourself
3) GOD—A promise you have made to God
4) A cross—A promise God has made to you
5) A hand—A promise someone has made to you
6) A heart with an "X" through it—A broken promise

Tell each student to roll their cube and respond by sharing a brief story that relates to the direction matching the word or symbol that landed face up.

63 *Trust Toss*

Tell kids to write down three things they trust others to do. Examples might include:
• Trust parents to care for me.
• Trust friends to keep a secret.
• Trust that Jesus died for my sins.
• Trust my teacher to be fair to me.

Tell kids to crumple up each trust into a paper ball. Gather around a waste paper basket and take large steps backward. On "go" have each student toss their trust balls into the basket, and sit down. Read the balls that made it into the basket and talk about how important it is to trust people with these things. Then gather the "balls" that missed and ask kids how they would feel if these trusts had been broken.

64 *Give it Away*

In advance: Fill two cups or cans with small objects such as plastic lids, coins, or wrapped candy. Each can should contain one object per child. Give two volunteers, called

"offering holders" one cup or can each as an offering can. Have the other children sit in a circle around them. Start the music and have each volunteer give all their objects to someone else in the circle. Those with the objects must keep one and hand the rest to a neighbor or put some back in the offering where the offering holders must give it away again. The children in the circle should try not to be caught with more than one item when the music stops. Repeat the game with two new volunteers as the offering holders.

65 *Penny Patience*

Divide the children into pairs. One child in each pair should be blindfolded and instructed to put one hand in a pocket or behind his or her back. Each pair will get 30 pennies in a plastic bag. When the leader gives the signal, the pairs should dump their pennies onto the floor. The child who can see must hold the plastic bag open but can do nothing else except encourage his or her partner. The child who is blindfolded must use only his or her free hand to pick up all the pennies and put them back in the bag as quickly as possible. When all the pairs have finished, switch roles. Then talk about the importance of having patience with others even when it is hard.

MEMORY VERSES

66 *Land Ho!*

In advance: For every two children, write a Bible verse or
phrase on paper. Use the same
verse or choose several with similar
word counts. Then print each word of
all the verses separately on small,
inflated balloons so the words aren't
readily noticeable. Scatter the balloons
around the room. Let the children pair
off and give each pair a paper with a
verse written on it. On the command
"Load Cargo," each pair will quickly gather the same number of balloons as words
in their verse and form a boat, sitting
with their feet together. On the command "Storm!" they
will read the balloons and throw "overboard" those not in
their verse. They will continue to gather and discard balloons as the commands are repeated until one pair has all
their verse words and shouts, "Land Ho!"

67 *Bible Verse Relay*

Write Bible verses on construction paper and cut them
into puzzle pieces. Divide the class into teams, depending
on how many members you want on each team. (There
should be the same number of team members as puzzle
pieces.) Line up team members and mark start and return
points on the floor. At the return point for each team,
place the scrambled puzzle pieces for Bible verses (one
verse puzzle per team). Each team member, in turn, goes
to retrieve one puzzle piece. The leader should call out

different motions that the kids must do while going to retrieve the puzzle piece—hop, twirl, skip, etc. When all puzzle pieces are retrieved, the team puts the verse together and sits down. The team must then memorize the verse together and be able to quote it as a group to the leader in order to win.

68 *Old or New?*

Make one flip card for each child from a 3" x 5" index card. Print "OT" on one side and "NT" on the other (make OT one color for all the cards and NT another color.) Write the names of the books of the Bible on another set of index cards for the caller. At the bottom of the card should be OT or NT to designate if the book is in the Old or New Testament. Also on the card should be a movement instruction (two baby steps, three hops, one giant step, etc.)

Line up all the children side by side behind a starting line and give each child a flip card. Choose one student to stand at the finish line and call out books of the Bible one at a time. After each book is called, children use their flip cards to display OT or NT to the caller. Those with the correct answer are told to move forward according to the movement instruction on the caller's card. The first child to reach the finish line becomes the new caller.

69 *Memory Verse Recall*

On a white board, draw a line for every letter of every word in a verse. Also include lines for the book of the Bible, but write the chapter and verse numbers. The verse below goes with the example on the following page.

"Commit to the Lord whatever you do, and your plans will succeed." Proverbs 16:13

– – – – – –/– –/– – –/– – – –/– – – – – – –/
– – –/– –,/– – –/– – – –/– – – – –/– – – –/
– – – – – –./– – – – – – – – 16:13.

Players take turns suggesting a letter of the alphabet. The leader should write the named letter in the proper spots. The winner is the player who correctly recites the verse and reference. Players are not allowed to guess until it is their turn.

70 *Bible Verse Delivery*

Have kids stand in a circle. After teaching a Bible verse, hand a Bible to one student and begin playing some music. Students must deliver the Bible to another player in the circle while the music plays. When the music stops, the person holding the Bible must say the next word of the Scripture verse, in proper order, or that person is out.

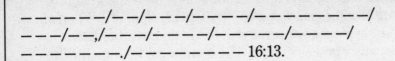

If the music stops during a delivery (while the Bible is actually changing hands), the delivery person must recite the first word, while the receiver then recites the following word. Continue play until the Bible verse has been completed or all but one person is out. If the last child can say the rest of the verse, he or she is the winner.

71 *Books of the Bible Pyramid*

Divide kids into several teams of three or four players. Give each team 66 small pieces of paper, pencils, 66 blocks, and some tape. Tell the teams to write each book of the Bible onto a small sheet of paper and tape it onto a block. (Provide Bibles for the kids to use if they do not know all the books of the Bible.) Then pile the blocks, pyramid style. The blocks must be stacked so that the books of the Bible are in order. See how high they can get the pyramid while keeping the books in order.

72 *Web of Words*

Say a Bible verse together several times. Then have everyone stand in a circle. Tie the end of a ball of yarn loosely around the wrist of the child saying the first word. After saying the word, the yarn is tossed to a second child. That child loops the yarn around his or her wrist, says the second word, and tosses it to someone else. Each time, loop the yarn around the speaker's wrist. Soon a web will begin to form. Continue in this way until everyone is part of the web. You may have to repeat the Bible verse to do this. To get out of the web, toss the yarn in reverse order, without the words. Or see if the kids can say the verse backwards!

73 *Chained Verse*

Divide the children into groups of two or three. Have each group choose different colors of construction paper and cut it into strips. Then they can write the words to the memory verse on the strips of paper. They can also add pictures or decorations that will make their strips easy to identify. Put all the strips in a big pile and have the children form one big circle around the pile. At the signal each group tries to find their own strips. Once they have all their strips, the children can use tape to put their strips together in a chain. The first team to complete their chain wins—or time the kids to see how long it takes for all the groups to finish.

74 *Memory Walk*

In advance: Arrange strips of masking tape to form a large circle according to the number of players. Make index cards with memory verses written on one side and the matching reference on the other. Place cards reference-side up in front of each strip of tape.

When the leader starts to play music, all players begin to walk around the circle. When the leader stops the music, all players stand on a strip of tape. The children look at the reference on the card in front of them. If they know the verse that goes with the reference, they raise their hand. The first child to raise his or her hand is called on to recite the verse. If the child is correct, he or she turns the card over so only new cards are used when the music starts again. The game continues until all cards have been flipped over.

75 *Fruit of the Spirit*

To help children learn the fruit of the Spirit, use masking tape to create a large "tic-tac-toe" board on the floor. In each square tape a paper with one of the fruit of the Spirit written on it. Form two teams, with each team standing in a line. Give everyone on Team A a hat to wear to distinguish them from Team B. The first person on Team A may stand in any square, then tell how that fruit can be demonstrated in his or her own life. For example, a child may stand on "patience" and say, "I'm patient when waiting for my dad to get off the phone." That child stays standing in that square. The first person on Team B does the same thing in a different square. Teams continue taking turns until one team has three in a row, as in tic-tac-toe.

76 *Go to Moses*

In advance: Make up a deck of Ten Commandment Cards, four of each commandment, for a total of 40 cards. Designs may range from just a single number on each card, to the text of the commandment written out, to a related picture or drawing.

Shuffle the cards and deal out five to each player. Place the remaining cards face-down in the middle of the table. Play the game just like a game of "Go Fish" where the object of the game is to collect groups of four matching commandment cards. Once a group of four matching cards is in hand, the player lays these down, face up, saying the commandment. Taking turns, players continue to ask other players for a particular card. If a player is asked for a card that is not in his or her hand, that player says "Go to Moses," and the asking player draws a card from the pile. Play continues to the left. The game ends when any player runs out of cards. The winner is the one with the most matching sets.

BIBLE REVIEW

77 *Bursting with Knowledge*

Write several review questions on narrow strips of paper. (You will need at least one question per child.) Roll each strip into a tight coil and slip it into a balloon. Use three different colors of balloons. Inflate the balloons and hang them around the room using colored ribbon and tape. Let each child choose a balloon and sit in three groups according to the color of their balloons. The teams should take turns popping their balloons and answering the question inside. Save the questions that teams do not answer correctly and give anyone in the group a chance to answer them at the end.

78 *Say What?*

Retell a familiar Bible story, but change several details. Each time the children catch an error, have them call out "Say What?" If they think they know how to correct your error, instruct them to raise their hands and wait to be called on. Once the children get the idea of the game, you can give them turns telling other familiar Bible stories.

79 *The Great Trade*

Make a list of terms you will be using in upcoming lessons. Include a simple definition for each term. (Examples: Eternal—lasting forever; Sin—willful disobedience of God's law; Gentile—a person who is not Jewish.) Write each word on a white slip of paper. Write each definition on a colored slip of paper. Mix up the slips and pass them out to the children. (Give each child a white slip and a colored slip.) Time how long it takes the group to correctly match all of the word and definition slips. As time and interest allow, continue repeating the activity to see if the children reduce the length of time it takes to correctly match all of the slips.

80 *Space Wars*

In advance: Mark spaces by taping the numbers one to ten along a wall. Write 20 Bible questions with answers on separate paper strips. Each question must have the same answer as one other question.

Divide the children into two teams. Have one team make a masking tape "X" on their shirts. The other team needs no markings. The teams will compete to have players in three adjoining spaces. Read a question to each team in turn. When answered correctly, that team will send one player with the written question to stand in the space they want to represent its answer. The space can be stolen by the opposing team whenever their question has the same answer. If one team gets both questions with the same answer, they can protect the space with two players and it cannot be taken by the other team.

81 *Scrambled Secrets*

In advance: (1) Make twelve mini beanbags: cut twelve 8" lengths of pantyhose, knot at one end, fill with one-half cup of dried beans, knot at the other end, and cut off extra nylon. You can substitute tightly twisted rubber bands for the knots if desired. (2) Write each letter of the alphabet on a paper square. Arrange the alphabet cards evenly on the floor to make a circle 7' in diameter and tape the cards in place. Place the bean bags in a box inside the circle.

Pass out a pencil, paper, and Bible to each child. Give the children three to five minutes to look through the Bible and choose a word of twelve letters or less. You could direct them to find people, places, or books of the Bible. The children write their secret word on their paper, and then write it again with the letters scrambled. The first "Secret Messenger" is the child whose own name is last alphabetically. He or she stands in the center of the circle and tosses the beanbags onto the letters of her secret word in scrambled order, looking at her paper for help. The other children stand outside the circle watching. The first child to guess the word being spelled gets to be the next Secret Messenger. Option for younger children: Use shorter words or have the messenger spell the word in the correct order.

82 Story Chains

In advance: Prepare several Story Starters, such as "The Flood," "The Exodus," "Jesus' Birth," etc. Divide players into two groups and have them sit across a table or room. A member of one group is given a soft ball and a story starter, for example "The Flood." This player must name something related to the story before the count of 10, for example: "rain." The ball is then thrown to a player in the other group who must name another thing associated with the word just given and the story starter. This player has to the count of 10 to come up with a related word or to pass the ball to someone in his or her group who can help out. No word may be used more than once. If a player fails to respond or reuses a word before the count of 10, the ball goes back to the other group. If neither group can think of a word, begin a new story starter.

83 Guessing Groups

Write names of people and/or places, from Bible stories that your group has studied recently, on slips of paper. Place the slips of paper in two baskets across the room from the kids. Divide the group into two teams and have a volunteer from each team cross the room to pick a slip from the basket. Volunteers return to opposite teams. The team members try to guess the place or person that was chosen by asking only "yes" or "no" questions. The first team to correctly guess what is written on the paper scores by adding the volunteer to their "guessing group." Play continues until all slips of paper have been used. The largest "guessing group" wins.

84 *Human Words*

On separate sheets of paper write words that correlate with a particular theme. An example of a theme is "Books of the Bible." Words that would work well are: Joel, Luke, John, Mark, Acts, and Amos. Another category could be "The Disciples."

Divide the group into teams so there are at least six children on a team. Give a team a word to "spell" with their bodies. They will work as a team to decide how to make the letters. Some letters might be formed best by two children. After a designated amount of time, the other team(s) are to name the word that they see formed. See who can guess the correct answer first!

85 *Picture That!*

The leader should prepare several small cards that each contain the name of a Bible story. Divide the group into two teams. One team begins by having one player select a card. That player will illustrate the story on a chalkboard

or large chart while the team members try to guess the story within one minute. If it is not identified, the other team has an opportunity to guess the story. A team point is awarded for a correct guess and that team continues with a new illustrator. If neither team can guess the story, play goes to the team that was not in possession.

86 *Fruit Basket Full*

Prepare a variety of 8 1/2" x 11" game cards and photocopy them. The game cards should have 16 squares (four by four) with a fruit of the Spirit written in each square. On slips of paper write brief descriptions of someone demonstrating one fruit of the Spirit. For example, one may read, "A child showing helpfulness." Place these slips in a basket. Distribute game cards and some fruit-shaped stickers to children. Pick slips from the basket and read them aloud. Players place stickers on the squares containing the fruit of the Spirit that matches the sentence that is read. When they have a straight line filled, players call out, "Fruit Basket Full!" Check to see that their boxes match the sentences you have read; if so, distribute new cards for the next round.

87 *Bible Spin*

In advance: Create an eight pie-piece game spinner. Mark each pie piece as follows:
• Spin again
• Answer two questions
• Lose 50 points
• Answer one question
• Answer one question and add 100 points to your score.
• Bankrupt
• Double your score
• Add 50 points to your score.

Prepare a set of questions to review your Bible story (or stories) on index cards. Tell kids to take turns spinning the arrow. Kids answer questions and follow directions accordingly. Score as follows: 50 points for each correct answer; minus 25 points for each incorrect answer. The person with the most points at the end of the game is the winner.

88 *Hit the Answer Spot*

Form teams of three or four kids and tell them to find a working area an equal distance from a designated "Answer Spot." Mark the Answer Spot on the floor with masking tape. Form riddles to review a Bible story. Teams must agree upon an answer and race to the Answer Spot. If the leader confirms that the first person at the "Answer Spot" has the correct answer, a sticker is awarded to that team. If an incorrect answer is given, that team loses a turn and cannot guess the next riddle. See how many stickers each team can get!

89 *Perfect Pairs*

In advance: Select some familiar Bible pairs such as Adam/Eve, Jacob/Esau, David/Jonathan, Peter/John, Paul/Silas that your group has studied. (You need a Bible pair for every two children—use some twice if needed.) Write the Bible names you have chosen on tape with permanent marker. Attach each piece of tape (with name on it) to the top of one apple. Place all the apples in a large bucket filled with water. Allow the children to select a partner and then bob for apples. The object is for each group of partners to get two apples that make a Bible character pair. Allow children to look for the apple they want in the water before going for it. If they get an apple that doesn't complete a pair, they must put it back.

90 *Job Hunt*

In advance: Tie two lengths of strong rope together in a circle that's large enough for eight children to fit around. Make a list of Bible characters that you have studied and their matching occupation. For example: Luke—physician; Joseph—carpenter; Dorcas—seamstress; etc. On index cards write only the occupations of these characters.

Divide children into four pairs. Have each pair stand around the circle of rope and grab onto it with both hands. Behind each pair, a few feet away, will be an index card with only an occupation written on it. When the leader says "Go!" the pairs will start a tug-of-war to move toward a card, but one hand must stay on the rope. Once a pair has gotten a card the leader calls "Time." The pair must say the job on that card and a Bible character who did that job. If they guess correctly, that card is thrown out and the tug-of-war begins again. If their guess is wrong, they must put the card back outside the circle and the tug-of-war starts over.

HAPPY HOLIDAYS

91 *A Reason for the Season*

Make a list of the holidays your church family celebrates each year. These might include Christmas, Epiphany, Easter, Palm Sunday, Maundy Thursday, Good Friday, Ascension Day, Pentecost, and Thanksgiving. You could include Jewish holidays if your children are familiar with them as well.

Collect small objects associated with church holidays such as: manger figure; star; lily flower; palm branch; communion cup; cross; cotton cloud; toy turkey. Arrange the collected items on a large tray. Have the children study the contents of the tray for two minutes. Then set the tray out of sight. Ask the children to name as many tray items as they can remember. List their answers on a chalkboard or chart. When they have listed everything they can remember, bring the tray out once again. Talk with the children about the holiday each object symbolizes.

92 *Holiday Scramble*

Cut shapes from construction paper in various colors, with at least two (preferably more) of each color. On one side of each shape draw or glue a picture of an object that is a holiday symbol. (These can vary depending on the holiday.)

Place shapes on the floor or on chairs in a circle configuration and invite children to sit on a shape. (You may want to secure the shapes with tape.) This game is played like Fruit Basket Turnover: The leader will call the name of a holiday symbol, and all children sitting on that symbol must get up, run to another shape depicting the same symbol, and sit back down. When the children run to a new seat, the leader must try to sit in one of the empty spots. The child left without a shape stays in the middle and calls out the next holiday symbol. When the child in the middle calls "Holiday Scramble" everyone must find a different shape to sit on.

93 *Christmas Sing-a-Song*

In advance: On several index cards write words that follow a Christmas theme: angels, Jesus, manger, stars, etc. Divide the group into two teams, have them face each other, and place the stack of index cards in between the two teams. One team begins by drawing a card. One player or the entire team has 15 seconds to begin singing a complete phrase of a Christmas song containing that word. The opposing team then has the same amount of time to begin singing a complete phrase of another song that has the same word. Play goes back and forth. A point is given to the last team to think of a song. The game continues with a new word with possession going to the team that earned the point in the previous round.

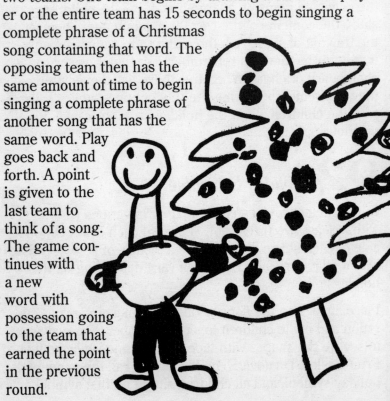

94 *Christmas Chairs*

This game is a variation of "Musical Chairs." Arrange the chairs (one less than the number of children) in a row. As you play Christmas music, the children walk around the chairs. When the music stops everyone tries to sit down. The child left standing needs to name a character or a fact from the Christmas story. A variation would be to have them sing part of a Christmas carol. Continue the game as time allows.

95 *Jesus' Diaper Bag*

Fill a bag with a stuffed donkey, straw, star, cloth diaper or rag, sheep, angel, gold, and perfume. Introduce the bag as "Jesus' diaper bag." Explain that it is filled with things that are part of the story of when Jesus was born. (You may also choose to dress and speak in character as Mary or Joseph.) As you tell the Christmas story, take out the items and display them.

After telling the story, put the items back in the bag and distribute paper and pencils to children. Give them a limited time in which they are to list as many items as they can remember.

96 *Thanksgiving Walk*

In advance: Tape paper numbers to the floor in "Cake Walk" fashion, one for each child, and put paper strips

with the same numbers as those on the floor, in a basket. The kids will walk around the circle while singing. When the leader rings a bell, they will each stand on the closest number. The leader will then draw three numbers from the basket. Children who are standing on those numbers have the chance to tell one thing they are thankful for. Each time a child's number is drawn and they share something, that child receives a dot sticker to place on his or her hand. Continue play until all children have had the chance to share.

97 *Great Gobs of Gum!*

This game is great with any holiday! Give each child a handful of bubble gum pieces and a paper plate. Set a figure of a holiday symbol (Christmas tree, Easter basket, etc.) in the middle of the table. The goal is to chew the gum until it is soft (one or two pieces at a time works best) then use it to make a copy of the holiday figure. Have the children race the clock to see who can make the best reproduction. Be sure to have wet towels handy to wipe off sticky hands!

98 *Holiday Draw*

In advance: Write some words related to any holiday on small pieces of paper. (Examples for Christmas: manger, donkey, Christmas tree, baby Jesus, gifts, etc.) Divide the children into two teams. A child from one team will pick a word from the pile of papers and begin drawing a picture on the board to get the rest of the team to guess that word. The team has one minute to guess what the word is. The child drawing cannot say anything. If the team doesn't guess, the other team gets one guess for that word. Whether they guess it or not, a child from that second team then gets a turn to pick a word and draw for his or her team.

99 *Jesus Christ Is Born*

Children stand in a circle, singing these lyrics to the melody of "The Farmer in the Dell." Choose one child to start the game as the shepherd. This child will start by following the instructions for verse one and continue throughout the song. Actions to accompany the lyrics appear in parentheses. You may want to read these aloud to the group all at once or as each verse is sung. (Hands are joined only during verses 1 and 4.)

1. Go, take your sheep and follow,
   Go, take your sheep and follow,
   Go, take your sheep and follow,
   Jesus Christ is born!
   (One player chooses two sheep, and they weave in and out of everyone's joined hands.)

2. Now enter in the stable, etc.
(Shepherd and sheep tiptoe to the center; others tiptoe in place.)

3. Now see the sleeping baby, etc.
(Shepherd and sheep still in the center, everyone "rocks a baby.")

4. Now go and spread the Good News, etc.
(Shepherd and sheep join hands and approach another player. This player joins hands as they move to the next player. Continue until all players are joined to form a chain. Repeat the verse if necessary.)

100 *Freedom Firecrackers*

In advance: Make two firecrackers out of construction paper cylinders with pieces of ribbon taped to the inside and coming out the top. One firecracker should be rather large (8"-10" tall) while the other is small enough to be hidden behind a child's back. Have all the children sit in a circle and close their eyes, with their hands behind their backs. Place the mini firecracker in the hands of one child and instruct the children to open their eyes but keep their hands behind their backs. Then select one student to come to the center of the circle to be "It." This child holds the larger firecracker and walks around the outside of the circle randomly tapping people on the head. When a child is tapped on the head, he or she must name one thing people can do in this free country that he or she is thankful for. If the child with the mini firecracker is tapped, he or she must chase the child who is "It" around the circle until he or she sits in the empty place in the circle. If caught, the child must sit out the next round.